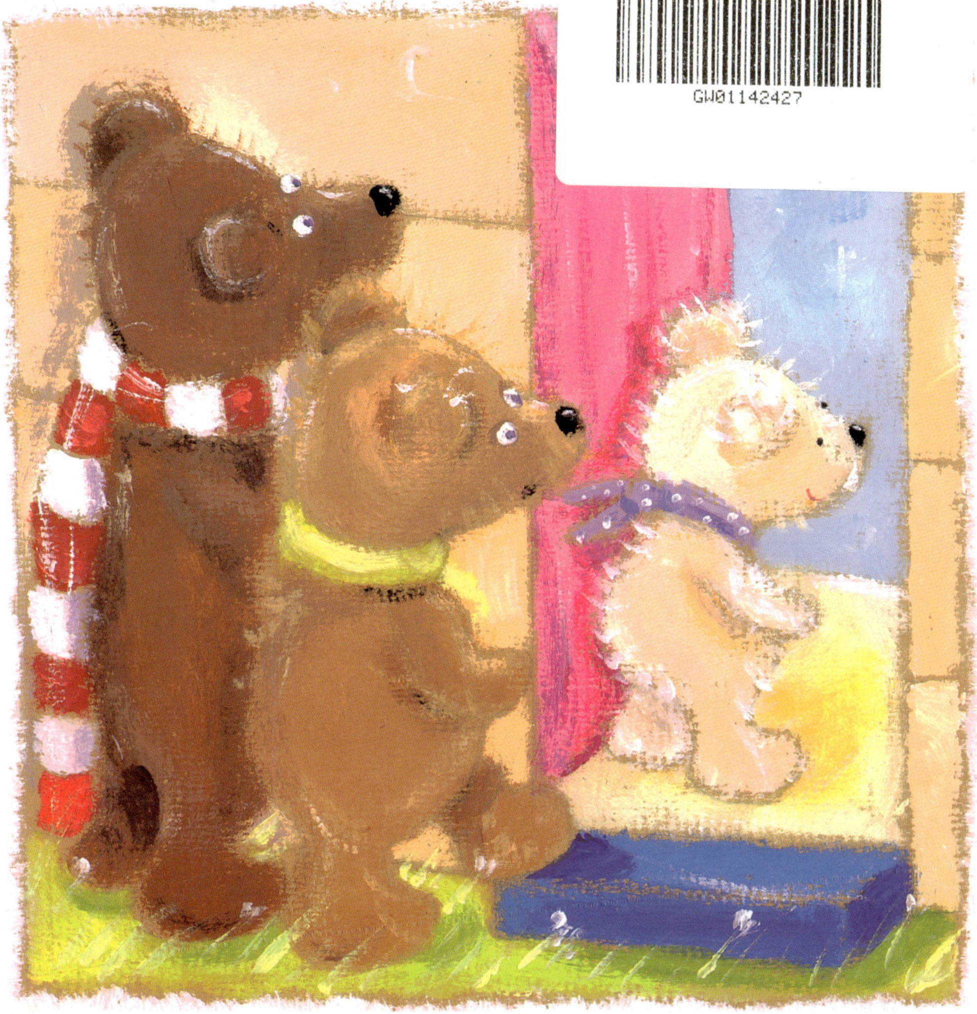

GW01142427

02263

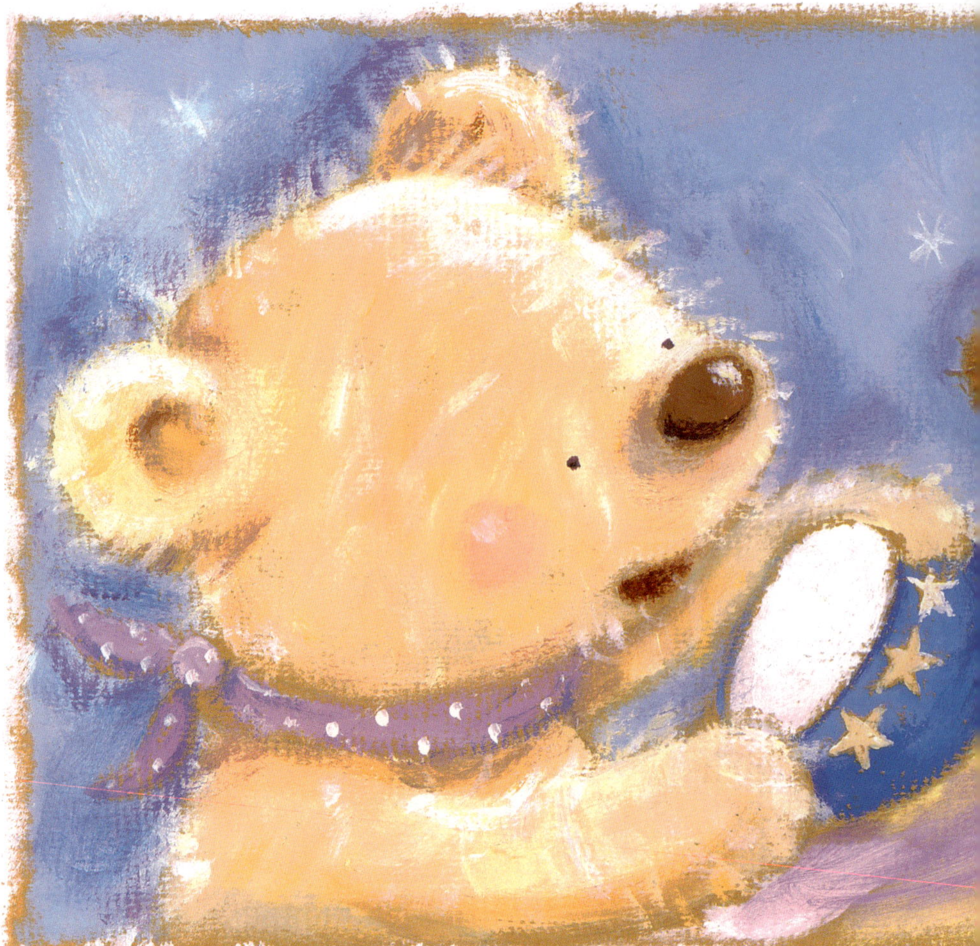

Somebody's been

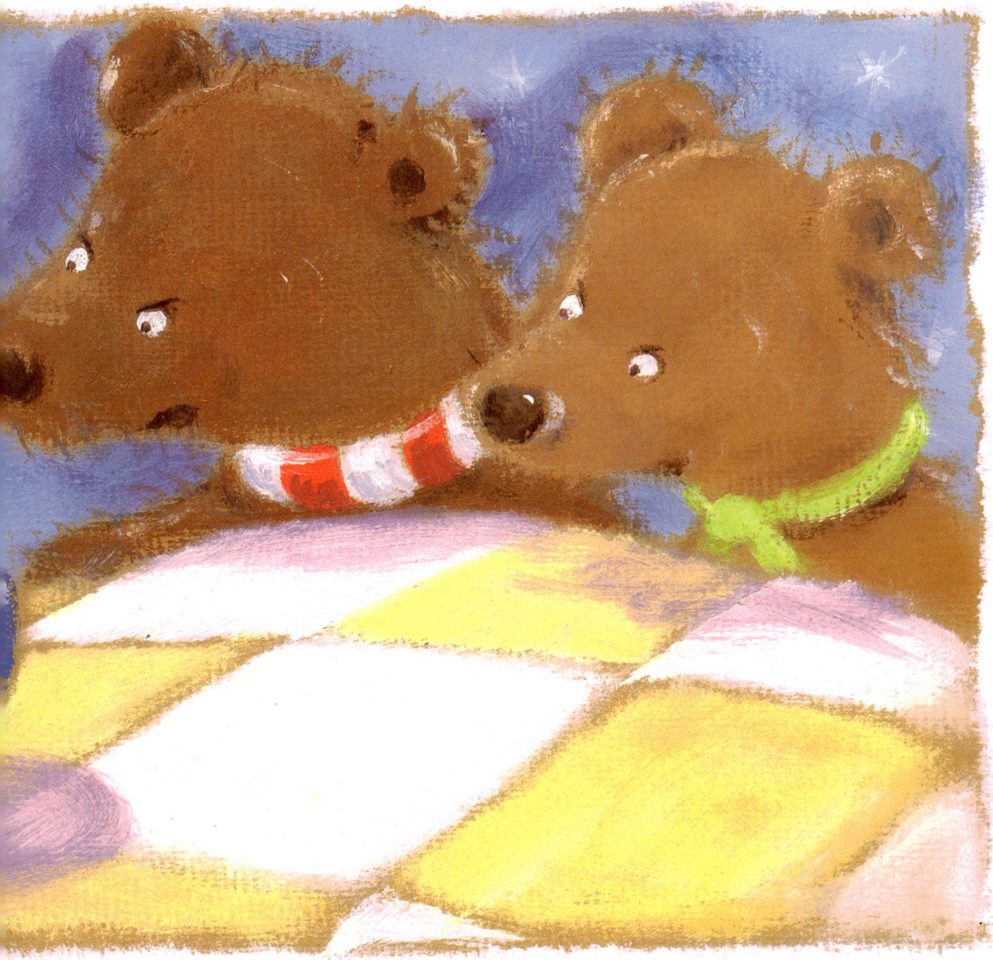

eating my porridge!

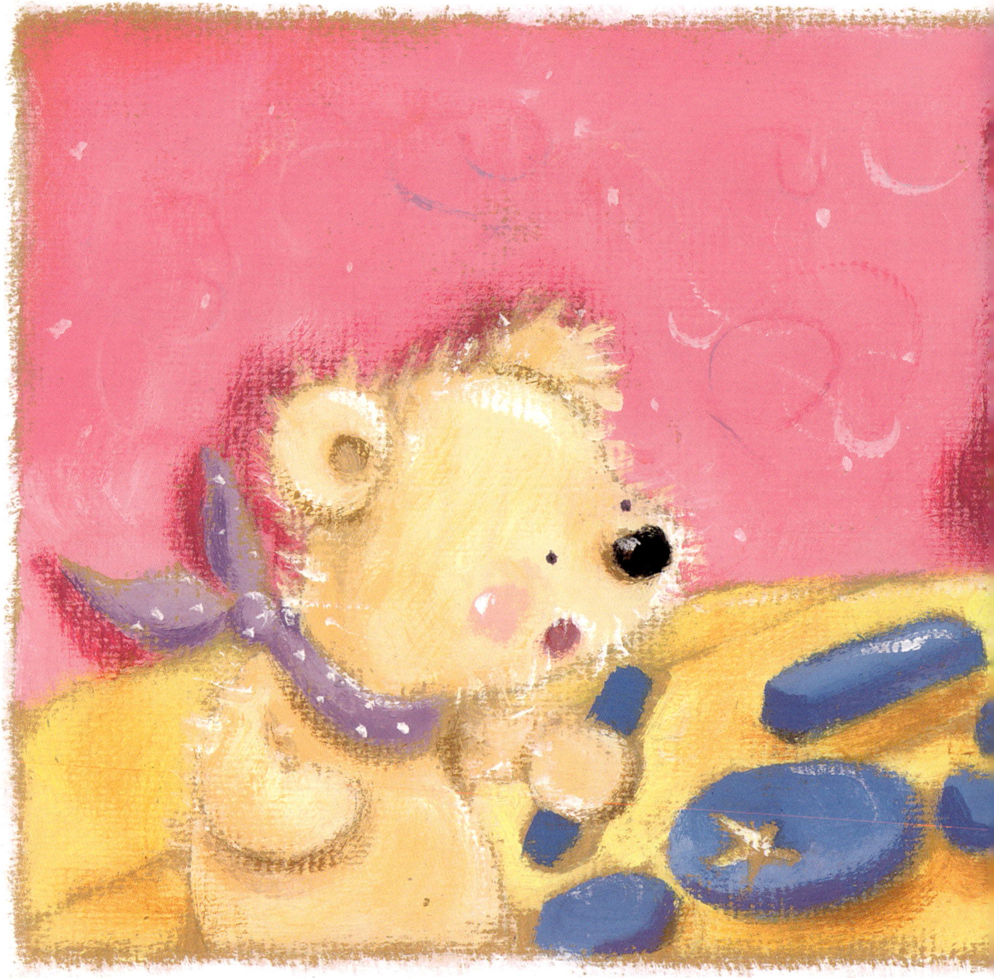

Somebody's been

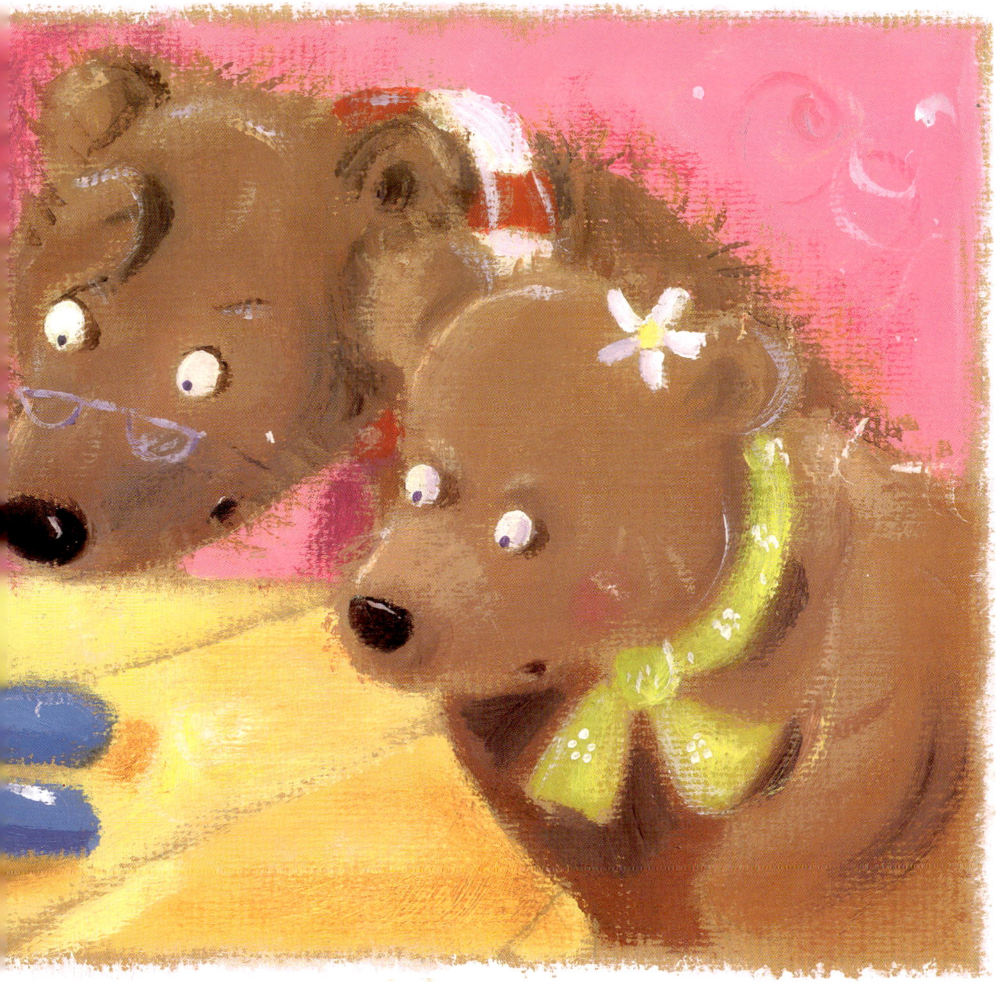

sitting in my chair!

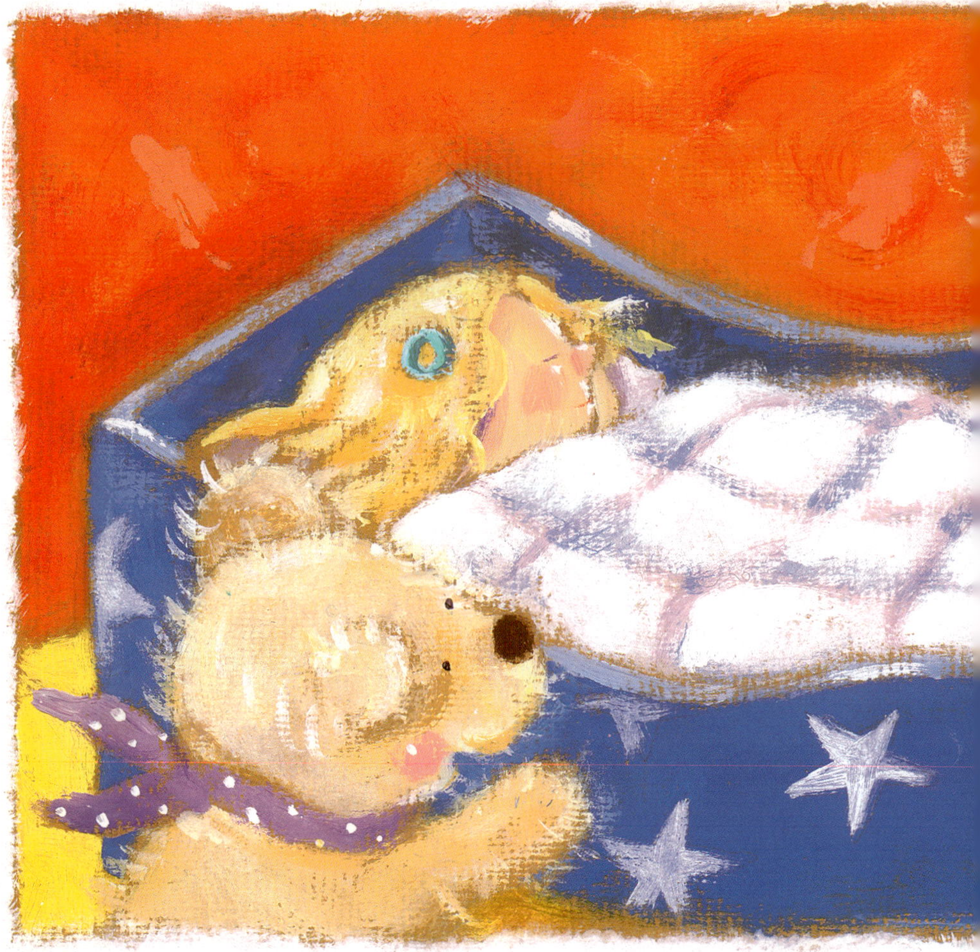

Somebody's been

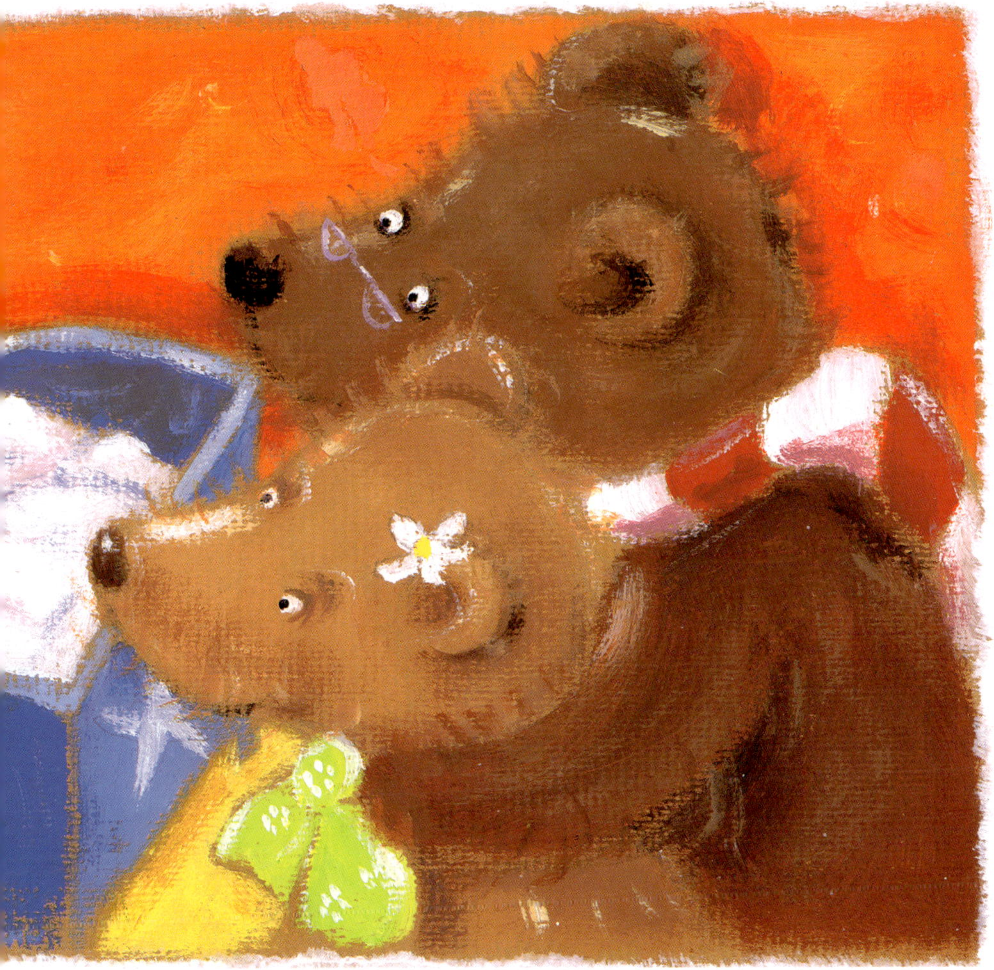

sleeping in my bed!

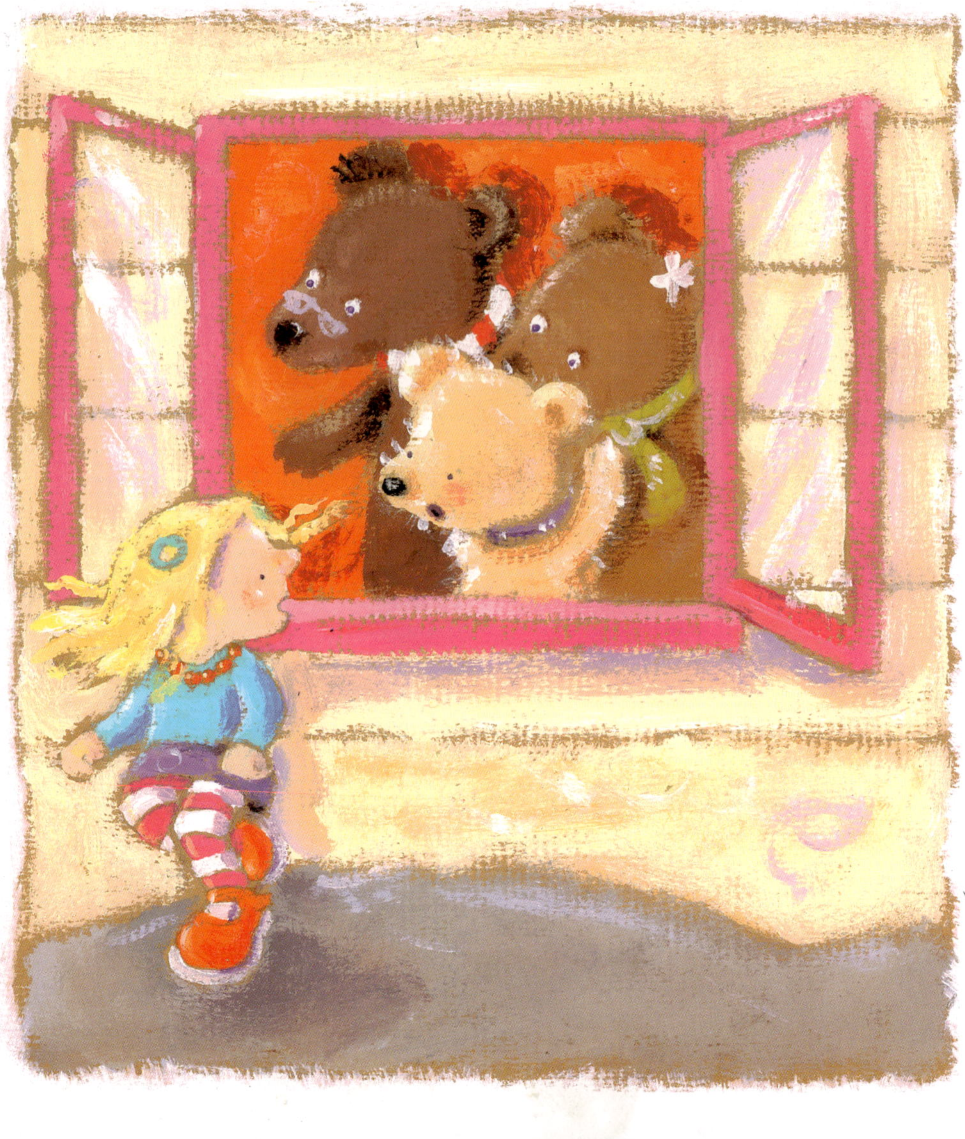